Let's Bring Them Up Sensibly

Let's Bring Them Up Sensibly

By Mae Carden

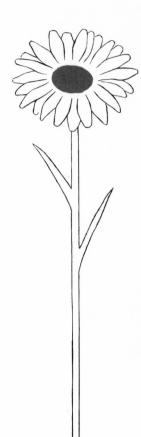

Published by
MAE CARDEN, INC.
1967

TO

The Students of the Carden Method who are striving to guide the children of America toward a full realization of their rightful heritage.

INTRODUCTION

"Let's Bring Them Up Sensibly" is being published in response to long-standing and oft-repeated requests for a Carden book for parents. The Carden System, developed and published by Miss Mae Carden, has long been recognized as an outstanding academic curriculum for students of all ages. This system is unique in that all subject matter is interrelated and sequential from grade level to grade level, and each of the hundreds of textbooks and teaching guides has been authored by Miss Carden herself. The Carden System is specifically designed to help children develop their innate powers of analytical and organized thinking. If followed correctly, this system will not only help the child to build a solid foundation for his academic pursuits, but it will also lead teacher and student alike to *life triumphant* because it is permeated in every phase with Miss Carden's never-failing cognizance of the unlimited potential of each and every individual being.

For those who have studied with Miss Carden over the years and who have experienced firsthand the joy and success of teaching by her method, there has been the delightful discovery that inherent in her teaching, though offered in light-hearted manner and with a liberal sprinkling of good humor, one finds a most perceptive and practical philosophy of life. Parents have pleaded to have at least some of this philosophy, this Carden way of life, in written form—hence, this present work.

Interspersed, as it were, with reading, spelling, grammar, arithmetic, geography, history, French, and Latin, this philosophy was originally presented in bits of wisdom, bon mots, or proverbs which seemed to make it particularly easy to accept, assimilate, and put to use; therefore, this little book is presented in like manner. You will find that the proverbs are arranged under sub-headings in a sequential order but that each one is independent and can stand alone. Inasmuch as we have found that these bits of wisdom have had to be applied in our *own* lives before they could benefit our children, we asked that Miss Carden include in this book guidelines for adults as well. Therefore, she has divided the book into two major parts: Part I "As You Act . . ." concerns the adult, and Part II ". . . So Shall You Guide" pertains to children.

It is our feeling that this volume can be a most valuable source of reference and inspiration for parents everywhere. Read on, and help your children to fulfill the promise of tomorrow. Let's Bring Them Up Sensibly!

The Directors of the Carden Schools

PREFACE

LET'S BRING THEM UP SENSIBLY is our title. What does sensibly mean? Does it mean rigidly? No! Does it mean without joy? Most assuredly not! Does it mean so practically that the imagination and the emotions are smothered? Heaven forbid!

Then what does it mean?

It means that the pattern of life is *Cause* and *Effect* and that the only way to assure the desired effect is to weigh life's values, bear them in mind, act in accordance with them, and reap the rich reward.

So many times the question is asked, "How does one learn to act in accordance with the law of Cause and Effect?" We offer this little volume in the hope that it will help you to realize the answer.

CONTENTS

PART I—"AS YOU ACT,......"

LET'S BRING THEM UP SENSIBLY

Part I

"As You Act, ..."

ALWAYS PLAY FAIR

Cause and effect is *fair* and inevitable.

———

One must "play fair" in *all* relationships.

———

Each one knows when he has not played fair and must pay the price, even if he won't admit it.

———

If one fails to play fair, he either tries to fool himself by justifying the act or lives with the misery of regretting the act.

———

The price for not playing fair is *the loss of inner peace.*

———

In order to play fair each person must be *honest* with himself —first, last, and always.

———

In order to play fair one must learn to look at life and relationships *objectively.*

GIVE YOUR MIND FULL CONTROL
OVER YOUR EMOTIONS

Do not be afraid to control your emotions. They won't be stifled; they will be more truthful, better understood, and in the long run far richer.

Your emotions, under control, can be used to embellish every experience in life.

———

Do not allow your emotions to be your master. If you do they will batter you to and fro with neither rhyme nor reason.

———

Uncontrolled emotions are always intruding and diverting the attention from the basic facts.

———

With his emotions under control, one is free to learn and to accept the truth.

———

Controlled emotions enable one to refrain from arguing when he is in the wrong.

———

With emotions out of the way you can be willing to admit it when you are wrong and have a sense of humor about it.

———

The person who has control of his emotions is willing to say "I am sorry" and make amends when he has made an error or caused an inconvenience.

———

Emotions should be a storehouse from which one draws to reinforce the drive to a given goal.

———

Don't humor yourself. The result offers no satisfaction.

Do not be the victim of different degrees of rage.

———

Control your temper! Say to yourself, "I must never be a part of a scene."

———

A display of temper is a misuse of emotion.

———

A display of temper is an adult temper tantrum. *Irritability* is its minor form.

———

Impatience is unbecoming. Be sure it is not due to lack of good planning on your part.

———

Do not give your wrath voice. Think before you speak.
"Now tell me what caused you to throw stones of unkindness into our calm stream of happiness? . . . Naughty children! You act like the dogs that slink through the streets and snarl at each other. Four horses cannot bring back cross words once they are spoken."
"Tales from a Chinese Grandmother"
Grade Five Class Book by Mae Carden

Controlling your temper does not mean that you are not disturbed by unnecessary annoyances, unnecessary delays, discourtesies, indignities, and frustrations of all sorts. It does mean that you have learned to evaluate their *relative* importance and to act accordingly.

If the various annoyances and frustrations are of momentary importance, they do not even deserve a comment, and it is most profitable to disregard them totally. If they are of somewhat greater importance, they can quite possibly be governed by a controlled comment. If they are of very great importance, they should be carefully considered and weighed, a definite conclusion should be reached and a plan of action followed. *Don't brood!*

BUILD A STRONG STAMINA QUOTIENT AND MAINTAIN IT

Stamina is mental staying power and endurance, and it must be built through self-discipline and faith.

―――――

Stamina rests on faith—faith in yourself and above all faith in God. Without religion, life becomes chaotic, and the soul is battered and bruised.

"For God hath not given us the Spirit of fear; but of power, and of love, and of a sound mind."
The Bible, II Timothy 1:7

―――――

Stamina which is strong dismisses fear, discouragement, indifference, unjust criticism, rivalry, cowardice, loss of self-reliance, envy, and sarcasm.

Stamina in the true sense enables one to establish convictions of Right and Wrong.

It becomes impossible to guide one's life along paths of truth when there is no conviction about right and wrong; all values become confused, and life loses all direction and purpose.

Do not let unbelievers mar your faith in life and in a Divine Ruler. There may be times when you feel that you do not have the words by which you can overcome the arguments used against religion, but in your heart you know that those who argue against God have lost the wise path of life.

When the subject of atheism versus God arises, listen only so long as courtesy demands it, then change the subject as quickly as possible.
"Let *not your heart* be troubled."
The Bible, St. John 14:1

Do not try to convince the over-articulate unbeliever. He is often armed with prepared arguments which must necessarily be only part truths.

"Things true and evident must of necessity be recognized by those who would contradict them."
Epictetus

Let those who disagree with you see that you respect the right of each one to his own opinion—but that it does not change your conviction. Your calmness will gradually reduce his fervor and may help him to reconsider his own viewpoint.

WHEN YOU ARE WRONG, CONCEDE IT!

Be honest with yourself in the estimation of your own acts, right or wrong.

———

Admit to yourself the emotion which prompted you to act in a wrong way. Name it. Was it jealousy, rivalry, aggressive pride, wounded pride, inability to praise the achievements of others, stinginess of soul, worldly ambition at any price, scheming—or plain deceit?

———

The minute you acknowledge the truth about your own wrong-doing, you will have an opportunity to face it, acknowledge it, plan a campaign against it, correct and then *dismiss* it.

———

When you have told yourself the truth about an unwise action, that little monitor, called your conscience, will then have a chance to take over and keep you from repeating the detrimental act.

———

When you have admitted the truth about your behavior to yourself and you have determined to eradicate the quality, *forgive* yourself, and start afresh. Add a prayer asking help in your undertaking. Regret will be banished. Self-pity will no longer hold sway.

———

Learning to forgive yourself will be a great help in learning to forgive others.

Everyone is entitled to at least two annoying characteristics. Are you certain that you have *only two?*

———

Remember that you are not going anywhere. Wherever you go, you take yourself with you, and therefore, you might as well make yourself pleasing to you.

———

Don't blame "life" for your failures. In every case you have caused the effect you receive, distressing as it may be. Logic would dictate, "Do not repeat the cause."

DEVELOP A SENSE OF HUMOR

A sense of humor is a most valuable character trait.

———

A sense of humor is built on a sense of balance—on a sense of relative importance. One has a sense of humor when one can look at a situation, see that one element is out of balance, and then be amused rather than upset by it.

———

Wisdom embodies optimism, not pessimism.

———

A sense of humor prevents one from becoming strained in relationships which could otherwise be annoying.

———

A sense of humor relieves so-called pressure and takes the strain out of life.

A sense of fun and of merriment adds flavor to life, but a real sense of humor is the great steadying force of life.

———

When did you last have a good laugh? Laughter is good for you. Laughter is refreshing.

SEEK THE REWARDS OF A HEALTHY ATTITUDE

Keep ever before you the fact that it is your attitude that determines your successes and failures in life.

———

Everyone has troubles. It is *attitude* that makes them a boon or a burden.

———

Don't waste one minute of your valuable life in doubt or fear. Watch your thinking!

———

You can do anything you really believe you can do.

———

Don't give up when difficulties arise or obstacles are placed in your way. Giving up is the great mistake. Always keep hoping and working for fulfillment.

———

Have a purpose in your life—not just wishes. Support your purpose with all your strength of mind and muscle.

———

Aimlessness results when the world is thought to control you. *You* make the world in which you live.

Do not trouble yourself about what others may say or think. Keep your faith in yourself, and your faith in God.

Socrates said,
   "He is richest who is content with the least,
   For contentment is the wealth of Nature."

Do not look upon the responsibilities which you must accept as stifling burdens. Build positive assets out of them.

Interest and effort will cure all your shortcomings.

The best things in life are free. Get out of the gutter. Keep looking at the stars.

Satisfaction is the feeling you experience when you have done something right.

The claim of having an inferiority complex is in reality the evidence of a frustrated *superiority* complex.

Intelligent people are never bored, because they can always turn their attention to some aspect of the situation which has value in it.

Keep life in proper perspective. Move back from the minor aspects of life and take a good look at the whole picture.

Quota your day. Do not let the routine of daily living dull your thinking.

"I can't" really means "I won't."

Will power is positive. It is based on stamina. Negativism is related to "won't" and will ruin your life experience.

Sustain your enthusiasm. The minute enthusiasm wanes, conviction and vitality depart and old age sets in.

RULE RIVALRY OUT OF YOUR LIFE

Rivalry should not be the motivating drive of your life. The motivating drive should be an intense interest in the subject.

It is intense interest that results in the consecrated devotion and unfailing enthusiasm that build the better product.

REFRAIN FROM SELF-PITY

Self-pity betrays self-centeredness and is destructive to the person who yields to it.

Look about you and compare your life with the unfortunate people. You will soon see that you have no cause for complaint.

When self-pity creeps in, turn your thoughts to helping others weather life's experiences. When you do, you will find a new joy in living.

———

Shy people are most often critical spectators. They cannot bear to expose themselves to the kind of criticism they use on others. Don't indulge shyness.

RECOGNIZE THE VALUE OF DIGNITY AND SELF-RESPECT

Follow the path that will lead you to being a better person, one for whom you will have respect and one with whom you will be satisfied to live your whole life long.

"To thine own self be true, and it must follow as the night the day, thou canst not then be false to any man."

Shakespeare

———

To develop and maintain self-respect behave *with dignity* at all times.

———

Dignity can be defined as "calm self-expression and self-respect."

———

Dignity has much to offer, because the kernel of dignity is *respect* and it presupposes self-control.

———

Dignity implies not only self-respect but respect for *every other person* as well.

Dignity is not established by authoritativeness or aloofness.

———

Dignity is reserve, but not withdrawal.

———

Dignity is being aware of the *real* values of life.

———

Dignity respects the personality of each and every person.

———

Dignity does not lack cordiality—in fact, true cordiality can exist only in company with dignity. Effusiveness and any atmosphere of camaraderie accompany informality and serve only to degrade. True cordiality reaches out to the recipient assuring him of his dignity and worth.

———

Dignity cannot be maintained without poise and the adherence to high standards in personal appearance, in manner of speech, in behavior, and in outlook on life.

———

Dignity commands respect.

———

If you wish to be respected, you must earn it. Respect cannot be demanded. It must be commanded.

———

People who command respect have something to offer in viewpoint, in personality, and in wisdom. You get the respect in life that you deserve.

———

Dignity includes self-control. *Self-control is the Lesson of Life.*

Self-control begins in your thinking. Dismiss tormenting thoughts; they are always unimportant. Replace them with purposeful thoughts.

———

Hold dignity as your shield against snobbishness. A personality which embodies dignity is never disturbed by snobbery.

AVOID THE CHARACTER TRAIT KNOWN AS SMUGNESS

Smugness is the quality which heads the list of *"Cardenal Sins."*

———

Smugness is the state of being contented with one's own minor accomplishments!

———

Smugness shuts out all growth, closes all conversation, causes mutual interests and friendships to wither, and reveals the lack of a sense of humor.

———

Smugness clashes with dignity because it is static, has no future, and lacks the valuable qualities which are embodied in dignity.

———

Do not wall yourself in to such a degree that you become bigoted, intolerant, and hostile to those who differ in their opinions. No matter by what name or reason this be called, it is smugness just the same.

———

Super virtue is slightly amusing!

Accept the fact that no one has yet demonstrated constant perfection. We all have *some* work to do!

———

Smugness obliterates true humility which is the solid foundation of every virtue.

BE GENEROUS IN THOUGHT AND DEED

Generosity is pure of heart.

———

"For God loveth a cheerful giver."
The Bible, II Corinthians 9:7

———

Generosity of spirit begets generosity in practical matters.

———

If you have spells of lack of generosity, dismiss them immediately. Force yourself to be generous, if you are not naturally so. Life has a way of returning what you give.

———

Stinginess of spirit is the second *"Cardenal Sin."* Stinginess is ego-centric to a marked degree. It cramps your soul and shuts out your friend.

———

Being generous *does not* mean being foolishly generous.

Being generous does denote an interest in the welfare of others and a discrimination in the recognition of values.

———

Generosity displays a delight in giving others a sense of well-being and a moment of fun.

Generosity carried beyond common sense is not a virtue. It does not show good judgment.

————

Generosity is an admirable characteristic, but a truly generous person does not permit anyone to *use* him. Nor does he give so much that the self-reliance and self-respect of those to whom he gives are endangered. Before that situation arises, the truly generous person will have withdrawn.

BEWARE OF INDECISION

Indecision takes one step forward and one step backward and leaves one just where he started.

————

Indecision breeds discontent, dissatisfaction, self-pity, and irritability.

————

Indecision irritates the onlooker, solves no problems, and prevents growth.

————

A wrong decision teaches a lesson. A correct decision strengthens the conviction.

————

Analyze the situation, weigh it wisely, and act upon your conclusion *without regret*.

CULTIVATE YOUR ABILITY TO QUALIFY AS A CHARMING COMPANION

A person is considered charming when he is a good listener and when he shows sincere interest in the interests of others.

A truly charming person is vivacious, courteous, and compassionate.

———

Take the time to be courteous. Courtesy is never optional!

———

Accept every courtesy gracefully—it is only courteous to do so! Refusal to accept a courtesy bruises the soul of the person who offers it.

———

You always impart what you *think* of life.

———

Always get to the point quickly in conversation. Long explanations are boring, and endless digressions are unbearable.

———

Avoid idle chatter because it is irritating to the listener and it belittles you.

———

It is said that there are three types of conversation:
1) about self—for those of little intelligence
2) about events—for those of greater intelligence
3) about ideas—for those of greatest intelligence.

AVOID COMPLAINING

Complaining is habit-forming. It devitalizes the atmosphere, is immature, and is never pleasant to the listener.

REMEMBER TO SMILE

A pleasant smile cheers the heart.

―――――

Don't glower at the world as it passes by; decide to smile instead.

―――――

Don't reserve your smiles for only your intimate friends. Fortunately, smiles are available in unlimited supply.

―――――

A smile assures the receiver that there are some people who are not hostile, not indifferent, not ungracious, not consumed by their own troubles.

―――――

The countenances of so many people seem to show self-disapproval. Do not let this happen to you!

―――――

You cannot conceal your thoughts. They are written on your face—so think better thoughts.

―――――

Keep your heart singing, and keep smiling—the choice is *yours* to make.

KEEP YOUR CULTURAL INTERESTS

Reading worthwhile literature will widen your horizon, develop your sense of values, enrich your experience, develop your vocabulary, and develop your powers of expression.

————

Keep reading classical literature, current literature, children's literature.

————

People read trash because their training has not rendered them capable of the weight of good literature.

————

Listening to worthwhile music elevates the spirit and inspires and fills the heart with idealism, lofty thoughts, and faith in the beauty of life.

————

Take the time to continue learning about art. Beauty wherever you find it elevates your thinking.

————

Above all seek wisdom. Information and knowledge may have some small practical value, but it is wisdom that begets enlightenment and understanding.

————

Watch your speech. You are judged by your diction and phraseology.

————

Do not use your age, your education, or your background as an alibi for poor speech. Correct your grammar. Grammatical errors can destroy you socially. Study and overcome.

In loyalty to your own viewpoint and convictions, you must become sufficiently articulate to explain and defend them.

A nasal quality of voice is irritating, and it lowers your cultural rating.

Overcome a nasal voice in this way:

Find middle *C* on the piano, find the *B* just below it. Then place your finger on the black note just below that *B—B-flat.* Keep playing the B-flat and recite a short poem, listening carefully to the pitch. Do it *three* times daily, and gradually that sound will get into your consciousness, and you will be able to tone your speech to it.

A pleasing voice costs nothing but *your* effort and time.

LET HAPPINESS BE YOURS!

Doing for others and *caring* for the welfare of others earn the reward for which the whole world is seeking. That reward is happiness.

A sincere interest in the welfare of others rests the soul and gives it time to recover from all its wounds.

Sincere interest in the well-being of others enables one to start afresh with renewed hopes and the renewed conviction that life is really a worthwhile, exciting, and rewarding experience.

Happy people are not happy just because they are doing what they like to do. These same people would be happy in most any field of endeavor, for they have developed the capacity to enjoy, to accept the necessary routines, to see beyond the obvious facets, and to bring forth greater significance in their undertakings.

———

Happiness is the by-product of doing for others.

———

"The happiness of your life depends upon the character of your thoughts."

Marcus Aurelius

ENJOY LIFE!

Enjoy the beauty of nature which surrounds you.

———

Enjoy the exquisite birds which should make your heart rejoice.

———

Enjoy the beauty of the sky, the loveliness of the flowers, and the charm of children.

———

Value the little experiences which make up your daily life and the kind deeds that you see others do.

———

Cherish the tenderness which kind people show to the weak and to the less fortunate.

Enjoy the success of others.

———

Turn your thoughts to the actions of the nobler people who have lived and are living. Do not expect to identify with them. *Let them inspire you.* Rejoice that such people live.

———

Appreciate those nobler people for the great ideas they have contributed to civilization. Unfortunately, it has become a rather fashionable pastime to try to tear down that with which one cannot identify. Do not be guilty of poking in bureau drawers in the name of history.

———

Appreciating the noble acts of others gives you assurance that *Life Triumphant* should be your goal. It has been achieved by many, and it does not have to be on a grand scale.

———

Do not believe that *so-called "life,"* which is really the *failure of life*, is the outcome of living.

———

Keep your thoughts on high ideals, and you will be surprised to find out how you will lift yourself and those around you.

———

All people want to be better and wiser and to progress in goodness and wisdom. How gratifying it is when, by your attitude and example, you can help them up just one step.

TREASURE THE SMALL PLEASURES OF LIFE AND EXPRESS GRATITUDE FOR THEM

The only people who are happy are the ones who are *grateful* for all the blessings that come to them.

———

A grateful heart is a generous heart.

———

Being grateful warms the heart and stirs it to share its possessions, ideas, and ideals with others.

———

When a person is grateful, he does not attribute his successes in life to himself alone. Therefore, he avoids the character trait known as *smugness*.

———

When a person is grateful, he is never the victim of pride, that deadly sin which permeates so many facets of life.

———

The cousins of pride are rivalry, vanity, avarice, egoism, self-centeredness, and other undesirable qualities. Pride attempts to destroy in others the very qualities which are deemed the noblest of all qualities: meekness, humility, and purity of heart.

———

"Gratitude takes three forms; a feeling in the heart, an expression in words, and a giving in return."
Distilled Wisdom—Montapert

———

Gratitude establishes within the personality a poise and a calm which in turn establish a sense of well-being.

A grateful person is at peace with himself and with the world. He smiles at the world, and the world smiles back.

———

A grateful person radiates contentment—not smug satisfaction, but a deep appreciation for what life has to offer.

———

A grateful person gives others the benign feeling that all is well and radiates a comfort to all who come in contact with him.

———

Gratitude does not limit. The real treasures of life come to the grateful for they know that wealth is not the goal of life, that fame has little substance, and that the inner life of each and every person is the all important facet of living.

———

Life has its own way of returning kindnesses, but not necessarily from the people to whom you have shown kindness.

———

You must not expect gratitude, or other reciprocation, for your acts of kindness. If you do, there will be no storehouse from which you will derive equal acts of kindness. The return of kindness always comes unexpectedly from other sources.

———

"Gratitude is the sign of noble souls."
Aesop's Fables

BE AN INDIVIDUAL AND RESERVE THE SAME RIGHT FOR OTHERS

No one can take the place of nor follow the exact pattern of another. Each one must travel his own path.

———

Search for the inner qualities of strength you see in others and develop those. Abide by your high *inner* standards. Be influenced by your *own* pattern of life. Grant others the same privilege, the same degree of freedom.

———

Being a "yes man" is a danger to avoid. "Yes men" are never interesting. The ideas they express are not their own. They are stereotyped and hackneyed.

———

Your own individual reactions have a freshness and a spontaneity which are pleasing to the listeners.

———

Stand by your convictions. What has happened to this country which was once regarded as the home of the rugged individualist?

———

Avoid the tendency to condition your opinion to the opinions of those around you.

———

Don't confuse judgment with opinion. You are not entitled to a judgment until your opinion has been proven right over and over again.

Opinions are too often *subjective* whims. Judgments are well founded and proven. Sound convictions are based on judgment, not opinions.

————

Develop some spunk! It gives you the courage to follow your own convictions. Do not allow people to trespass.

————

Those who create on their own never stoop to tamper with the work of another. However, listen to men of good will and to those who demonstrate good living. Analyze what they say and do. Your recognition of their strength will help you to grow in your own individual way.

LEARN TO RECOGNIZE THE TRULY SUPERIOR PERSON

The truly superior person is one who embodies the finest elements of character and disposition.

————

The basic characteristic of the superior person is *empathy*. In practice empathy is an application of the Golden Rule.

————

A sense of empathy banishes criticism of others, develops compassion, banishes gossip, and proves your love of your neighbor.

————

The truly superior person has the mental and emotional development to understand the viewpoint and needs of others.

————

Superiority does not flaunt itself. It is apparent!

The truly superior person has the "understanding heart" which enables him to utilize his academic knowledge and his insight into life's values for the good of mankind, which in turn enriches his own life.

The superior person always treats the other person as he would like to be treated.

The superior person remembers that the so-called *simple things* of life are really the *most profound* and are so deep that they cannot be penetrated in one life-time. Therefore, he gives the *simple* things of life daily study and daily appreciation.

REJECT SNOBBERY IN ALL ITS FORMS

Snobbery is merely an expression of *over self-evaluation*.

The total disregard of humane values inherent in snobbery automatically destroys the value of associating with a snob. One who seeks friendship with a snob will find nothing but a valueless, will-o-the-wisp relationship.

Remember that no one can hurt you but yourself. You can only be snubbed by your own consent.

Remain true to yourself and be not disturbed in the presence of those who seem not to respect you. Why should you accept *their* estimate as final?

"It is your own fault if you accept an insult."

Chinese Proverb

———

There is a tendency to excuse snobbish behavior on the grounds of insecurity. In reality it is the result of the low evaluation of another and the dismissal of that person because he or she offers no personal advancement to the snob, whose only aim is social advancement.

———

Social patronage is a form of snobbery. When a person is guilty of showing patronage to a fellow-being, he is guilty of being *discourteous*.

———

There is no place in our social relationships for the lack of courtesy.

———

There is certain immaturity in social patronage. The person who is guilty of this discourtesy feels superior; but alas! he is exhibiting contempt, a quality of inferiority.

———

The so-called sophisticate is a snob, too! The aim of the sophisticate is to *dazzle* those who lack a similar sophistication.

———

Sophisticates may have acquired knowledge, but they have certainly not digested it.

———

That which is real need never be "shown off."

Sophisticates may have acquired "savoir faire," and they may know just how to behave on all social occasions, but they have lost the human touch.

———

When a person's manner assumes the state of *strutting*, he is indulging in childish behavior.

———

Differ if you will, but do it politely.

———

Don't give audience or response to that which you find offensive. Ignore it, and change the subject.

———

A genial smile or laugh will always do much to restore the calm which has been destroyed by argument.

———

How tragic it is to see one who has had academic training and opportunities in life *bruise* the feelings of those who have not had the same opportunities! Hasn't this so-called intellectual failed to realize that every human being has something to offer? Hasn't he thereby earned the more accurate title of pseudo-intellectual?

———

The pseudo-intellectual appears to be bent on proving the statement that "a little knowledge is a dangerous thing."— True knowledge is knowing how little we know.

———

"All of our knowledge is but a handful of pebbles on an illimitable shore."

Isaac Newton

When a person, who has been given the advantages of fortunate opportunities and academic training, assumes a sense of superiority and the right to insult or patronize others, he has proven unworthy of his own good fortune.

———

A supercilious remark always expresses a lack of self-control and a lack of wisdom.

———

A *sense of privilege is the great curse of living.*

BE A GOOD NEIGHBOR!

"Love your neighbor; yet don't pull down your hedge."
Benjamin Franklin

———

Neighbors will not try to run your life if you are dignified.

———

Over-familiarity invites advice from neighbors.

———

Be friendly with your neighbors, but maintain the line of distance. Over that line no one steps. It is an invasion of your privacy.

At first neighbors may seem to resent a distant attitude on your part; but in the long run you will have their respect; and there will be no barriers preventing true neighborliness.

———

Don't let people walk on you. It makes you dislike them and yourself.

———

Informality has great lure on the surface, but it is fraught with many pitfalls, many unexpected disappointments, and many embittering experiences and is therefore not a wise procedure at any time.

———

"Familiarity breeds contempt." An old adage, yes. Alas, 'tis true!

KEEP FAMILY AFFAIRS IN THE FAMILY

Financial affairs, family worries, the ages of adults, and criticism of adults within the family should never be topics of discussion with children or with outsiders.

———

When you criticize your family, you prove yourself to be disloyal, self-pitying, and lacking in good taste!

———

Do not give advice. Most people who ask for advice are asking only for a confirmation of their own opinion.

———

If you find yourself giving advice, stop. You are only irritating the other person.

Do not ask personal questions of others. They are both irritating and out of place.

———

Do not discuss your physical problems. No one is really interested, and when they are told and retold, it lessens your dignity. ———

Keep your personal affairs to yourself. Keep your conversation on subjects of general interest.

DO NOT INDULGE IN GOSSIP

Do not say unkind things about people. You never know their inner life.
    "Judge not that ye be not judged."
                                    The Bible, Matthew 7:1

———

When people make derogatory remarks about acquaintances, it is wise to say, in response, "I have never seen that side of him."

———

Keep your thoughts above the *petty*, and your words cannot reflect pettiness.

———

Do not repeat unkind remarks. They are like weeds. They spread so quickly that they are soon out of control.

———

When someone reveals facts to you in confidence, do not relate these facts to others.

Do not expect others to keep a secret which you have been unable to keep.

BE A GOOD FRIEND

Welcome pleasant acquaintanceship with most people.

———

Treasure your few friends.

———

Those who like all like none!

———

Do not mistake civility for *friendship*. It is apt to be good manners — quite devoid of personal approval.

———

Do not imitate the modern tendency to be a self-appointed psychologist who analyzes the actions and motives of his friends.

———

"Give therefore thy servant an understanding heart. . . ."
The Bible, I Kings 3:9

———

Only God knows the inner working of each soul, and each is holy ground. Never trespass!

———

The only way you can be of real help is to be the embodiment of finer attributes.

Your example will speak louder than words.

You expect others to grow. Will you? You often hear this remark, "I have always been this way." That means that no growth has taken place.

The quality of empathy is the core of pleasant personal relationships. It is based on good will and is expressed by acts of consideration.

Do not mistake empathy for an indulgent attitude which refuses to face reality. Empathy does not lack a sense of discrimination; it includes discernment.

Empathy is positive, practical, and down-to-earth in spirit. It moderates criticism and widens horizons.

Empathy awakens one to the fact that each and every one in the world is really alone.

No matter how many people surround you, you are *always* alone.

The greatest help that one human being can offer to another person is filling a personality need.

Unhappiness often results when one expects another person to ease the soul, which is something only God can do. You must not expect friend, family, or mate to remove the sense of being alone. That sense of aloneness is the longing for communion with God. The human soul is lonely and dissatisfied until peace of mind is found by this communion with God.

LET'S BRING THEM UP SENSIBLY

Part II

"....... So Shall You Guide"

KEEP A WELL-KNIT FAMILY LIFE

The home should be the gathering place for the family. It should not be a railroad station from which each member goes off in a different direction.

———

Family ties need to be strengthened, not loosened. These ties do not bind. They offer a common interest which endears each member to all the members of the family.

———

The dining table is the *center* of the family life. When all the members of the family gather together at meals, a bond begins to knit the group. This bond should be consciously nurtured by the parents and treasured by every member of the family.

———

The father should assume his position as head of the household with dignity, setting high standards of behavior in every way.

———

The father's position in the home can be likened to that of president, while the mother takes a position rather similar to that of the supreme court.

———

Policy should be discussed and *settled* between the parents *before* it comes up in the presence of the children.

———

The father, as head of the household, should be the one to ask the blessing before meals.

Table conversation should be agreeable and as interesting as possible. A variety of reactions should be accepted, providing the differences of opinion are expressed in courteous language.

————

During family discussions it most often falls to the mother to temper the degree of opposition and interpret the varying viewpoints. She must keep the harmony and help the younger members to word statements in courteous language.

————

Meals should be balanced. They should be served at regular hours, and the family table should not be a short-order lunch counter.

————

At the family dining table the *mother* should be seated first and should assume the position of the hostess.

————

The mother should be the homemaker. She may have some outside interests, but her home and her family should always be of utmost importance.

————

Many children are suffering from their mother's over-absorption in herself and in her life outside of the home.

————

A well-functioning home has to have a capable organizer at the helm.

The routine of family life should be systematic. When the daily routine is maintained efficiently, there is time left to pursue varied and individual interests.

———

Children should be expected to contribute to the work required in simple household chores, meal preparation, serving and clean-up, and the various activities in the home that provide for the comfort of all the members of the family.

———

This work should be distributed fairly according to the ages of the children. The unwilling members of the family should be required to do their share. The affable members of the family should not be expected to do the work of unwilling members of the group.

———

When a mother says that it is easier to do it herself, she is failing as a parent.

———

Parents are expected to teach their children how to live. It is only by the daily exposure to and application of high standards that children can build the habit of living with a purpose and establishing a wise pattern of behavior in a family situation.

———

When the mode of family life is not producing the desired results, it is up to the parents to stop, analyze the situation, admit their errors, and develop a new daily procedure, a new efficient routine, an improved philosophy of living.

Children need a calm environment in order to thrive. They need a little free time to collect their thoughts. Therefore, children should not be expected to run to an after-school lesson each day. They should have a few opportunities, but they should not be pushed on to appointment after appointment. Such a busy schedule is exhausting and creates nervous tension.

It is not wise for either the children or parents to rush from one interest to another.

Parents should plan to offer entertainment at home as well as outside of the home, and they should be willing to give up some of their own entertainment, if necessary, during this time of the child's life. Simple refreshments please the youngsters. The family room (or living room, if there is no family-type room) should be a place to play games which the young people like. If the youngsters like to dance, radios and record players should be a part of the equipment.

Parents should know what is going on, but they should not try to be a part of the entertainment.

Slumber parties are a dangerous form of entertainment. They offer little but the opportunity to become over-tired and to pick up undesirable habits and information. They cannot be properly supervised.

All children should be taught to be gracious hosts. Give them the opportunity to practice receiving guests, taking their coats, making them comfortable, and initiating suitable conversation.

Little girls should be taught to sew, to crochet, to knit. Their skill should be improved until they have such understanding that they are able to use these skills easily and independently.

––––––

Little boys should be taught the use of the hammer and saw. They should experience the joy of making serviceable objects.

––––––

Little boys and girls should be taught to garden and to take care of pets.

––––––

Children should be taught many skills that will serve them in a practical way.

BUILD A STRONG SENSE OF FAMILY AND ITS RELATIONSHIPS

It is the *role of the parents* to establish the family unity. It can never be done by pressure.

––––––

Family unity will be lasting if the mother and father "play fair" with each and every member of the group. *Parents must not play favorites.* If they do, antagonisms which are apt to last a lifetime, will develop between the children.

––––––

Family interests, excursions, outings, and experiences strengthen the bonds which unite a family.

––––––

A child gains security when he feels that he is an integral part of a group. It gives him that comforting sense of belonging, and he gains the assurance that comes as a result of being included.

Grandparents should hold a place of honor within the family.

It is wonderful for a child to have the opportunity to spend time with his grandparents; however, grandparents should not allow themselves to be regarded as babysitters.

Children are the responsibility of parents, not grandparents.

Rejoice if your child can enjoy the company of his grandparents. They can teach a child so many wonderful things.

If God had wanted to, He could have removed all the old people from the earth, but He left them here to give wisdom to the younger ones. Seek that wisdom and cherish it!

Do not leave your child with babysitters too frequently. When it is necessary to leave your child, select your baby-sitter with great care. Not only the child's life, but his thinking as well, is at the mercy of the one who is caring for him.

GIVE CHILDREN THEIR RIGHTFUL PLACE WITHIN THE FAMILY

The eldest child should be treated with the courtesy due his right of birth.

The first-born must not be pushed aside for the younger children.

The eldest child should have the opportunity to spend some time with his parents when the younger members are not included.

The eldest child should be given privileges not yet given to younger members of the family.

Each child should have to wait for a given age to receive certain privileges. The youngest child should not be allowed privileges ahead of his years.

Gifts for the first-born should not be duplicated for younger members.

Do not use the oldest child as babysitter for the younger children. There may be times when it is absolutely necessary, but do not make a habit of it.

Children do not have the maturity to meet a crisis should one arise; therefore, responsibility for the lives of others should never be placed on them. In the event that a tragedy should occur while he was in charge, the child would never forget it. Children thus used could very possibly carry a life-long burden should this happen.

A lifelong burden of guilt would be a terrible price to pay for a few moments of pleasure or convenience.

The youngest child should not be permitted to usurp the attention which belongs to other members.

When age is the gauge for all privileges, the parents are not accused of playing favorites.

Both Mother and Father should make every effort to treat each child with equal respect and affection.

Parents must not show favoritism. No home is happy where favoritism is shown.

Parents should not speak of the comparative abilities of their children. The children are well aware of their relative abilities and do not need to be told about them.

Parents should remember to be kinder to the adolescent. He is still half child, yet he is competing with the adult.

People are very indulgent with the cute little fellow who needs to be spanked, but they are mean to the adolescent.

Parents should make a special effort to make the teenagers feel that they are very important members of the family circle and that the parents are always interested in their activities and problems.

Sibling bickering should not be tolerated at any time. It is destructive to both parties and results in a tendency to lose sight of the relative importance of relationships.

———

Parents who brag about the ability and achievements of their children embarrass their children with adults and create animosity with other children.

———

Do not seek popularity for your children. As a rule, popularity means lowering your own standard to please the lower standard of other people. Popularity means the loss of real individuality.

———

Never make a scene! Always protect your child's dignity as well as your own.

BUILD YOUR OWN STAMINA

Make an effort to make your own stamina strong. The child knows it when you think one thought and guide with the opposite action.

———

If you are afraid, you will teach fear to the child.

———

If you lack strength of conviction, your child will know it, and its influence on him will never be to his advantage.

———

A person who loves a child never permits him to do less than his best.

Remember that each person is as good in life as his interest and his stamina.

ASSOCIATE WITH YOUR CHILDREN AS A PARENT

Being a good parent is the most important job you can do, and it is a most rewarding experience.

––––––

Do not be a pal to your child. You cannot be both a parent and a pal.

––––––

Your child wants you to be a *parent*. To maintain a healthy relationship, the adult must be treated with respect by the child.

––––––

If parents want their children to respect them, they must practice what they preach, be just, be consistent, and really love them. Empty words of affection will not be accepted by the children.

––––––

Many parents mistakenly believe that they can bind their children to them by humoring them, by making excuses for misbehavior, by breaking sane health rules, and by endless indulgence. These parents do not understand the needs of a child.

––––––

Children love those who help them to meet life.

Children are grateful to those who have cared enough for their future to make them rise to the best that is within them.

———

Children appreciate the warm understanding of those who have made them strong enough to control their weaker sides and to rise to a level they could not have attained by themselves.

———

Parents should not be taken for granted by children. The children should appreciate the love and protection which their parents give them.

———

Children should not be permitted to speak discourteously to their parents at any time, nor should they be allowed to speak in a derogatory manner about *any* adult.

———

Without actually stating it, the parents should awaken the child to the realization that the best friends the child has are his parents and his grandparents.

———

If a child respects his parents, a word of approval and confidence will do more toward building a fine character than all manner of bribes or rewards that could have been offered.

———

It is impossible to make life easy for your children. Each child must meet his own problems. Therefore, the most important thing you can do is to equip him to do so.

It is not necessary to give your children all your time. Generally speaking, quality is more valuable than quantity, but always try to be available at important times.

———

Do not think that it is enough to give your children a hurried embrace and kiss as you hurry off to your own interests. You will become almost a stranger to them. Why should they obey, respect, or have confidence in that kind of a parent?

———

Tucking a child into bed at night is one of parenthood's most valuable privileges. It is a time to build a natural bond of closeness; it is a time for taking stock of life in general, for telling stories, for confidences, and for prayer. Do not deny your child this security.

———

Complaining is as bad a habit in children as it is in adults. To counteract it, establish the bedtime practice of reviewing "only the good things that have happened today."

———

Stop the complaining! Counter it with, "Tell me two good things."

———

When your children are telling you of their experiences, it is wise to ask them to include at least one thing that was especially nice and also one kind or courteous thing that they have done for another.

Children tend to tell you about their experiences when they are fresh in their minds. Be at home when your child arrives home from school whenever possible. Be sure to be available after special parties and games. Be prepared to *listen* and to give wise counsel.

———

There are many areas in which it is necessary to counsel your children. Here are some of the problems that seem to crop up most often and various suggestions for solving them.

Jealousy and Rivalry

Point out:

That no one can take another's place, and that there is plenty of room in the world for everyone.

That each one has something different to offer the world.

That he is showing lack of the self-respect which God expects of him.

That he must learn to be true to himself and develop himself in the light of his own gifts.

Injustice — expressed as "not fair" by the child

Point out:

That many times people do not play fair. (Do not deny this. It is a fact!)

That he must learn to be a person who does play fair so that he can have self-respect, gain the admiration of others who play fair, and set an example for those poor souls who do not know that fair play is the best way.

Retaliation, Revenge, Resentment

With a gentle approach:

Let the child tell you what he would like to do.

Let him get the venom out of his system.

Ask, "Do you think that would help?"

Say, "Isn't it nice that you know how to behave better than that?"

Let the child talk on. Then ask, "Do you feel that you could do something better with your time?"

See that he gets started on something, and then, drop the subject!

Injured Feelings — due to rude remarks

Say:

"That *was* unkind. Now you see what you should not do. Don't you think that it will help you to be kinder?"

Children should learn early that rude remarks have no ability to hurt anyone unless one allows them to do so. In fact, rude remarks are much more injurious to the one who lowers himself to that level of behavior.

Injured Feelings — due to the lack of an invitation

Discuss the fact that we never know the other fellow's reasons for inviting one person and not another, but that chances are if your child is being a desirable type of companion, he will be included next time. In the meantime, point out that there are many other possible interests for that time, and let him know that you consider him capable of finding one and pursuing it *happily.*

When there is any meanness involved in not sending an invitation, handle it as any other rudeness.

Do not give him a substitute party. It will not help him to meet disappointments.

Discuss each incident objectively and let him see both sides. Do not imply any criticism of his actions; he will sum up the situation.

———

Parents should not get involved in the petty quarrels of children. To the children they are very important for a few moments. However, they are soon forgotten, and the children are playing together again.

———

If a playmate proves to be an undesirable companion or an untrustworthy playmate, sever the acquaintanceship. Do not prolong the discussions — just stop the association!

———

Jealousy, anger, a feeling of injustice, resentment, retaliation, and revenge can destroy confidence and reason, affect the nervous system, and often upset a child's speech. Parents should be alert to perceive and recognize these attitudes when they are present. They should give the child an opportunity to talk about his feelings and thus rid himself of the emotional disturbance, without fear of censure or blame.

———

It is sometimes necessary to help a child free himself from destructive emotions. How much wiser it is to discuss them than to allow them to burst forth in violence.

A child should feel free to talk over all his problems. Parents should be sympathetic but should help him to meet his problems objectively and to rise above them. Again, the parent lends the child stamina while the child builds his own.

Conversations between parents and child should be held in trust and never referred to again.

Parents should never refer to past mistakes, to past, unpleasant experiences, to confidences. Many lives are made miserable when this sin is committed. Don't be guilty of it.

Parents should not act shocked at questions that are asked or attitudes that are stated. The parents' contribution is to help the child to establish the relative importance of various experiences.

Children who talk over their problems with their parents when they are young are apt to continue to seek parental comment and help as they grow older and are in need of guidance from their parents. Begin early!

Remember that nearly all experiences which seem very upsetting and annoying at the time have a tendency to fade away in importance.

Parents should help children to evaluate the relative importance of experiences. The unimportant and the trivial should be dismissed, and the important experiences should be discussed.

———

Parents should call on the child's sense of humor. Many times a laugh will cure what otherwise might seem a major tragedy.

———

The parent, who will help his child to grow strong in body and in character by holding the child to the highest standards possible for him, and who adds to this adherence to standards a sincere interest and faith in his child, will receive devotion and affection that will last all his life.

GIVE YOUR CHILD THE BENEFIT OF GOOD TRAINING EARLY IN LIFE

"Train up a child in the way he should go: and when he is old he will not depart from it."
The Bible, Proverbs 22:6

———

The child establishes his pattern of life during his first year. He proceeds by trial and error to take his place within the family group.

———

If a child finds consistency, firmness, and affection in the family procedure, he adjusts himself to that outlook on life.

If a child finds that he can dominate the family life because of inconsistency, indulgence, and absence of firmness, he will proceed with the following patterns of behavior: temper tantrums, disregard of the given order, resistance to directions of any kind, lack of consideration for the rights of others, saucy retorts which will be excused on the grounds of fatigue, illness, or the unfair behavior of others. Restlessness will prevail!

This child will be notionate about his food, his rest, his playtime, and will be criticized by the onlookers.

Will this child be happy? No. He will be a discontented person.

Will this lack of training equip the child to meet social situations? No.

Will this lack of training prepare the child for school life? No.

Children who are brought up this way can almost be guaranteed to start school in Group 3.

―――――

Success in school life and, I dare say, in all of life, requires self-control, awareness of the rights of others, fair play, and a willingness to be taught.

―――――

Strive for the characteristics of poise, controlled behavior, willingness to be guided by an adult, contentment, playfulness, an awareness of the rights of others, a sense of humor, self-respect, pleasant social relationships.

Children who have these characteristics have parents who based their early training on the deep desires of the child. They knew that the child was expecting the parent to establish the bounds on which he could function with security and with happiness.

Be consistent in dealing with your child, and keep ever-evident your *expectancy of good.*

———

Parents who indulge a child one day and punish him for the same act the following day encourage undesirable behavior on the part of the child. Unless the parents change their ways, both child and parents will remain frustrated.

———

Many children are suffering from over-posessiveness on the part of the mother. An over-possessive mother stifles the child. She destroys the child's self-respect. The personality of a child who is submissive by nature is crushed. The stronger-willed child will develop an animosity toward the mother. There is no real happiness in a home where the mother is over-possessive.

DISCIPLINE YOURSELF TO DEMAND OBEDIENCE

Obedience is immediate, or it is not obedience.

———

Parents should bear in mind that they must not be charmed into indulgence by the young child.

They must realize that he is trying people out, pushing as far as he can push in order to establish where the boundaries of acceptable behavior lie. Children know instinctively that within those boundaries they can feel secure. Do not deny them that security.

———

Why do children obey? Because it is *useless* not to!

Parents should not be indulgent. If they are, they will raise spoiled children.

————

Do not think that you are making anyone happy when you permit disobedience. Onlookers are disliking the child and criticizing you. You are merely indulging your own weaknesses.

————

Direct the child, but don't order him about.

————

Raise children who obey not through the control of a strong hand, but through an understanding of cause and effect. (You do this and that happens, and *no one* can stop it.)

————

When a parent gives a child a command, the child should obey the command immediately. This command does not need to be expressed in hard, stern tones. It is a command, even if it is given in a gentle voice, and should be recognized as one.

————

Parents should not give too many commands. They should not nag. When they give a command, however, it should be followed by obedience on the part of the child.

————

Training should be given in carrying out two or three commands in sequence. Children have great need of learning to respond correctly to verbal directions. This training develops concentration which is needed for success in their school work and in life situations.

To test the degree of listening on the part of the child, children should be required to repeat several commands which have been given to them orally before performing them. As soon as the child proves that he is able to carry out several commands, the repetition is not required.

———

When you give a command such as, "Pick up your toys," be sure that you follow through and see that, either under his power or yours, (with whatever attendant disciplinary actions are needed), he *does* pick up his toys.

Beware the common pitfall of giving punishment as an alternative which then allows the child to avoid obeying the command.

———

Do not give punishment as an alternative to obedience. Do not say, "Do it or I shall punish you." Recognize that even with punishment the command was not obeyed. Instead say, "You *will* do it either under your power or under mine (with whatever suitable punishment), but you *will* do it." This way obedience is not optional.

———

A child does not resent having to obey. In most cases he is seeking the bounds within which he will feel free to act. A parent is failing the child when he does not establish these bounds for the child.

———

If the child is naughty and needs a rebuke, make the child realize that you still love him, but that his *act* is not acceptable.

It is much better to make a child be obedient than to allow him to misbehave until you are "out of patience."

A child does not resent a firm slap when he oversteps the bounds after sufficient warnings. A cruel word or a lashing glance will bruise his soul. He is not given to forgiving them.

A parent should not feel guilty after he has punished a child for misbehavior. The act had to be stopped for the welfare of the child. Remember that any path of misbehavior that the child might follow can end disastrously.

Parents who maintain a balanced viewpoint and the light touch or a good sense of humor, can help nearly any situation.

A fault-finding mother destroys the happiness of a home. Many times she is blaming the children for her own shortcomings.

Fault-finding is often the result of frustration.

Fault-finding is often the result of unwise parental guidance which has not been successful.

Parents who over-sermonize will not improve any situation.

When the child does show improvement in his attitude, say, "That is a better way." Do not make it personal by saying, "You are behaving better." This statement embarrasses him. The statement about the behavior is impersonal. It helps the child to be objective.

————

If parents indulge the child, he will not love them. In his heart he knows that he needs discipline to help him. A child is made of firm clay. He wants to measure up to life. The child gives his love and gratitude to that person who helped him achieve his goal.

Oh, Parents! Please do not deny your children obedience;

For if you deny them obedience, you deny them courtesy;

If you deny them courtesy, you deny them deference;

If you deny them deference, you deny them reverence;

And if you deny them reverence, you deny them the ability to achieve their full stature, because they will never know humility.

HELP YOUR CHILD TO BUILD STAMINA AND SELF-CONTROL

Life is an experience in which a person must strive to prove himself able to meet all the problems that come his way without being embittered or discouraged and to have the moral fiber to turn them to his advantage.

———

Parents who deny the infant and the toddler the training which will develop self-control on the part of the child are certain to develop into naggers and frustrated human beings.

———

Parents should not coddle their children. Expect each one to walk alone. Help them to grow strong.

———

Being stern when a child shows weakness is not showing a lack of sympathy. It is helping him to live up to a standard he could not maintain on his own. Help him to build his stamina until he can stand alone and meet situations.

———

The Stamina Quotient (the S.Q.) is the most important quotient in life. Being mawkish about a child is giving the child the wrong impression of life. Life is not an unbroken series of pleasant experiences.

———

If you are not in control of your emotions, then you are not in control of your mind.

To help a child gain physical control, teach him to sit still. Have him watch the clock for one moment while he sits quietly, without moving. Gradually increase the time one minute at a time — up to five minutes. Suggest a subject for meditation as he sits quietly. Every child needs to have the ability to maintain his self-control in this manner, and unfortunately it does not always come naturally.

Children should not be left alone for long periods. Too often this leads to undesirable habits.

Threats of harm to the child should not take the place of obedience.

The parent should be aware of emotional fears which can disturb a child, and should help the child to overcome these fears as soon as they become apparent.

Fear of the dark or fear of being alone should not be allowed to develop. If a child shows any sign of this fear, the parent should remain at a nearby distance and talk back and forth to the child. Gradually the parent gets farther away. If the child feels that he can depend on his parents' constant interest in his welfare, this fear will gradually be overcome.

Fear of thunder and lightning is a frequent problem. One cannot say that there is no danger; lightning does strike at times. Give comfort and reassurance along with instruction for safety measures.

When a child is frightened, do not deny the danger. Help him to meet it, take all possible precautions, and then dismiss the subject. The parent or an adult can divert the child's attention with a story or an activity. Certainly, a comforting arm about the child is a proven help.

Parents should name a destructive emotion whenever they see one in action. They should treat it objectively and encourage the child to discuss it. By so doing they may give him the help he needs to control it and finally overcome it.

Do not make promises. Discuss the possibilities of outings and activities, but make the decisions in the light of the family needs at the time.

Do not let children express disappointments by pouting, sulking, or making rude remarks.

Do not let the children get their own way in order to make up for disappointments. Life is full of small disappointments, and a child must learn to meet and overcome them.

Keep working to develop the child's sense of humor. It will be invaluable in the acquisition and maintenance of self-control.

In many cases physical fear results from a lack of muscular tone. The child should be guided to develop muscular strength. Added to strength is the need of physical balance. When the child acquires muscular strength and balance, he gains a sense of confidence which prevents physical fear from developing.

KEEP PHYSICAL DEVELOPMENT IN
PROPER PERSPECTIVE

The health of the child should be carefully watched. Anything that impairs a child's health impairs his ability to live a full and happy life. Physical problems should be detected and corrected as quickly as possible. Where correction seems impossible, every means of comfort and a hopeful and positive attitude should be adopted.

Physical problems should not be accepted as limiting, but they should be corrected where possible.

Mothers should make certain that the child's *sight* and *hearing* are in good condition. Many difficulties in school arise when problems with these senses are uncorrected.

Children must have enough hours of rest. The nervous system of the child pays the price when the child has an insufficient amount of sleep.

An over-tiring schedule threatens the child's ability to function emotionally and academically. It is most assuredly not fair to teacher or student.

The bedtime should be a set time. There should not be nightly arguing about the bed hour.

Children should rise at a given hour in the morning. Lying in bed encourages laziness. Hurried dressing and a hurried breakfast give a poor start to the day.

―――――

When an occasional festivity delays the bedtime hour, a nap should be taken on the following day.

―――――

Correct posture plays an important role in good health and in personal appearance. Exercises to develop correct posture for the child should be done daily.

―――――

The parents should provide equipment and games which will help the child to develop both large and fine muscle control and coordination.

At an early age they should teach him to hold and use a teaspoon (not a baby spoon) *correctly*. This will avoid difficulty with a pencil later on.

The child should learn to use a pair of scissors efficiently. He should learn to use a crayon. Children should be given more and more opportunities to use scissors for increasingly difficult cutting. Be sure that left-handed children have scissors that are specifically designed for them.

―――――

The parent should teach a child to clap and tap rhythmically.

―――――

The child should be taught to use a ball—to roll it in a given direction to a given spot, to bounce it a given number of times, to throw it and catch it.

The child should learn to pedal toys—simple forms of bicycles.

The child should be taught to swim at an *early* age.

The child rejoices as he masters physical requirements. The parents should show interest and pleasure in the child's achievement, but they must avoid *exaggeration*.

The child should acquire a sense of balance. He should learn to run, skip, hop, jump, jump rope, roll hoops, and balance himself on boards.

If a child is timid, critical comment should be avoided.

The parents should help the child make progress step by step. The parents should remain relaxed and encourage the child, giving him comfort and assurance by the remark, "Wasn't that fun! It did go better today." A hug of assurance or a pat on the head reassures the child and helps build his physical stamina. Discouragement must not be allowed to develop in any area.

Achievements should be gradual. A child should not be expected to perform complicated feats until he has built up to it by mastering simple feats.

Faith in the person who is guiding his physical development must abide in the child's heart.

Parents should be very interested in the child's progress, but physical prowess should not be given an importance it does not merit.

Do not discuss a child's achievements or the lack of them before the child.

Differences between the achievements or abilities of children should be considered normal daily occurrences in the development of physical fitness.

Resist the temptation to make remarks about comparative achievements of the children in your family or in other families. Children are well aware of their comparative abilities.

The purpose of physical training should be the development of the physical stamina to support his mental stamina, thereby fully developing the child. Its goal is not competition or rivalry. Competition may be considered at a much later date, but it is incidental to physical achievement, not the purpose of it.

If the only reason a child goes to school is to beat the fellow next to him (be it physically or academically), what happens when that other fellow moves away?

SET HIGH STANDARDS IN EVERY AREA OF LIFE

Standards within all aspects of family life must be established and maintained, if the family is to succeed as a family. There should be standards of appearances, behavior, speech, conversation, housekeeping, and of individual service to the family welfare.

ESTABLISH HIGH STANDARDS OF BEHAVIOR AND MAINTAIN THEM

You teach what you are.

———

Do not expect your children to be honest if you ask them to lie for you when you do not wish to accept an inconvenient telephone call, or when you wish to purchase a less expensive ticket to the movie.

———

Establish rules of order and formality.

———

Formality is a better way of life. Respect for the rights of others is an inherent part of formality.

———

Formality is important to children because, like discipline, it gives them security. It gives them the knowledge of the boundaries of acceptable behavior and, therefore, the opportunity to be comfortable within them.

———

Never let a sarcastic word cross your lips, and never make a coarse remark.

Do not allow children to be on equal terms with adults or to have equal say with them. Children do not have the experience to make judgments, and when you intimate that they do, it is very upsetting! It destroys their confidence in both present security and future progress.

———

Both adults and children must be courteous. Rudeness is neither acceptable nor permissible *at any time!*

———

Pouting in the young child should be stopped. It grows into surliness and finally into downright rudeness.

———

Sauciness should be stopped. It grows into impudence and eventually into sarcasm.

———

Self-centered behavior, which always includes lack of consideration for others, destruction of property, or some kind of self-indulgence, should be discussed and stopped.

———

The child needs to become aware of his responsibility to the family welfare, to the school welfare, and to life situations.

He can soon be made to realize that he must learn patience.

He must realize that needless crying is not acceptable.

He must realize that he has to entertain himself at times, and that he cannot have the constant attention of adults.

———

A child can soon be taught to play with his toys instead of hurling them about and demanding that they be returned.

When he reaches the toddling stage, the child needs to learn that some objects are his, while other objects belong to others and must not be touched.

Give a very young child an opportunity to touch objects under supervision so that he may become acquainted with different textures, weights, and substances. After this opportunity has been given, teach the child to see and sense with his eyes as well.

Do not permit a child to have "cheeky fingers." Develop his power of the "tactual-mental."

ESTABLISH STANDARDS OF APPEARANCE THAT REFLECT THE DIGNITY OF MAN

Slovenliness should never be tolerated.

Slovenliness has many modern names. Extreme dressing has no place at any time.

Individuality is not increased by disregarding high standards of dress. Low standards in dress certainly fail to indicate any individuality of character.

Have you ever seen a slovenly bird? Birds are never slovenly; neither are the flowers!

If parents want the respect of their children, they will have to keep up their own standards in every detail.

Parents should set the example for their sons and daughters. Children are always estimating adults.

Remember that children are more critical of their parents than the parents are of them.

Mothers cannot command respect unless their appearance is above reproach. Mothers who do not maintain a high standard in their own appearance will not command the respect of their children.

The highly prized sun-tanned state is only *skin* deep, while the lack of dignity in many costumes reveals flaws in the character. This truth cannot be withheld from the children.

Recoil from the repulsive expression, "Let your hair down." Anyone loses dignity when he makes this statement. It indicates two-facedness and that either the formal you or the informal one is a fake.

Be your natural best at all times. Do not wear a mask which you long to remove.

A child's personal appearance should meet the standards of cleanliness, neatness, and appropriateness for the occasion.

In the earliest years the child must have his clothing selected for him, but as soon as he is able to understand, he should be told which clothing is appropriate for the various occasions, weather, and activities in his experience, and he should be made aware of tasteful styles, color combinations, and patterns.

By the *age of seven*, the child should be ready to be given the choice of selecting the garment he wishes to wear from his collection of clothing.

The mother should be commenting on the relative durability of the garments. Vanity should be avoided.

By the *age of ten*, the child should be ready to begin to select the garments he prefers to have purchased for him, under guidance and within a given price. The mother should be giving the child an awareness of the variety of clothing needed and the budget required.

By the *age of fifteen*, the boy or girl should begin to purchase independently the garments needed. A sense of values, good taste, and an awareness of the budget should have been firmly established by this time. If they have not been, make haste! There is not much time left for such training.

HELP YOUR CHILDREN TO REALIZE THAT COURTESY IS NOT OPTIONAL

Children should be required to act courteously.

———

If formality is required on all occasions, the children will acquire good manners and use them constantly. Good manners are not mechanical responses.

Every child wants to be treated with respect, but he must earn that respect by the superiority of his attitude and behavior.

———

Children should acknowledge the presence of anyone entering the room by greeting them. If an older person enters the room, the child should rise to his feet and remain standing until bidden to be seated.

———

Prepare your children to use proper greetings for children and for adults. "Good morning" and "Good evening" are the gracious greetings. "Hi" is not the greeting for persons older than yourself. "Hello" is for the telephone. The answer to "How are you?" is "Well, thank you."

———

Children should be required to listen whenever anyone is speaking to them. They should be required to give their full attention to the person who is speaking.

———

Children should be taught to make some pleasant remark to the people they meet, and they should be instructed in the art of initiating and carrying on conversations with various types of people.

———

Children should be taught to be aware of anything they can do to be helpful and to offer any courtesy which is needed.

Children should be taught at an early age to refrain from staring at or commenting about people who have handicaps. They should be taught to see and not comment until they reach home. At that time the parent explains the problems which some people have to face. In pointing out the courage shown by those who are less fortunate, the parent awakens sympathy for the handicapped and helps to develop a gentle, considerate attitude on the part of the child.

Do not permit a child to contradict. It is ill-mannered. If he does it, have him apologize immediately.

If a child hears a wrong statement and has the urge to inter-rupt or contradict, ask him which is wiser—to be rude to someone and hurt his feelings or to let the mis-statement go?

The child will make the correct choice.

Explain to the child that he is going to hear many, many mis-statements, that mis-statements do not alter the facts, and that he should just be glad that he knows the truh. Teach him to have a sense of humor about it.

Do not allow children to interrupt. Teach them, that if it is necessary to break into a conversation, they should *quietly* get your attention and *wait* to be recognized *before speaking*. Be sure that at such times you return their courtesy and recognize them as quickly as possible. Only in an *emergency* should children verbally break into a conversation.

It is so easy to teach children the little courtesies that add pleasure to life if you will just remember to tell them what is the nice thing to do and then appreciate and enjoy it when they put your suggestions into practice.

Teach a child to accept graciously all courtesies. His acceptance will encourage the one who has offered the courtesy to continue being courteous.

GIVE YOUR CHILD THE ADVANTAGE OF GOOD SPEECH

A pleasant speaking voice is a million dollar gift for your child.

If the ability to express one's exact feelings in words were a universal achievement, there would be no ulcers and far less disagreement in the world.

The ability to communicate well is a most valuable asset. As adults we have an *endless* number of people with whom we must communicate in order to carry out the rigors of every day living. Even the young child needs to *communicate* with his parents, the other children of the family, friends, and neighbors.

Parents should make every effort to equip the child with clear diction (pure sounds of a, e, i, o, u), correct pronunciation of words, approprite phraseology, fluency of speech, an accurate vocabulary, and, as the child develops, an extensive vocabulary.

Teach children to talk. Begin early and build sequentially. Do not accept purposeless chatter.

———

Parents should help their child to relate little incidents in sequence.

———

From his early childhood teach a child to speak in a well-modulated voice.

———

Give your child every opportunity to speak with clear diction and with clarity of thought. If he needs help, provide a teacher for him.

———

If the child is given a large vocabulary, he will not be limited to slang terms, and he will not keep repeating the same word over and over again.

———

Extensive reading will enable a child to gain a discriminating use of words.

———

A larger vocabulary will give a child a wider scope of experience. It will equip him with the power to communicate his reactions and his opinions. It will give him the capacity to enjoy using words himself and the ability to appreciate the clever use of words by writers and speakers. It will enable him to convey shades of meaning. It will make him discriminating.

———

A child with a fine vocabulary will not be limited to trite, obvious, and often brusque remarks.

The development of a speaking vocabulary is a *parental* responsibility.

Words are the vehicles by which people express their thoughts.

As soon as a child has mastered a vocabulary of the first level, the parents should consciously use words of the second level, giving the definition before using the word.

———

Parents should create an excitement about acquiring a large vocabulary. They are not encouraging the child to become a pedant; they are widening his horizons.

———

The use of words can never be developed in a dogmatic way. It must be done with delight.

———

Impatient parents often silence children who might be learning to communicate. Over-talkative parents destroy the child's desire to speak.

———

Parents should not talk down to children. They should use an adult vocabulary and define the words in simple language.

———

If the parents are interested in words, they can expect that words will become important to their children as well.

———

Slang should be avoided. The children will hear it outside the home. They will know it, but they do not need to use it.

Objectionable language should never be used; it is the product of *low* thinking. Parents should be above such abuse of their responsibility to their children.

———

Do not consult children regarding subjects on which they have not developed the right to an opinion. Do not encourage children to offer their opinions when adults are discussing subjects with which the children are not acquainted.

———

Self-centered conversation should be avoided. Most often it can be curtailed easily and nicely if you will just change the subject. If the child is discourteous enough to continue, take him aside and explain what he is doing and how discourteous it is.

———

Children should be cautioned against repeating any gossip or personal information. Thoughtless people will sometimes attempt to lure information from the child. Do not put him through that experience.

———

Parents should not discuss the personal affairs of other people before the children.

———

Private family affairs should never be discussed before the children. They do not have the judgment to remain silent.

———

Children should not chatter about family affairs. Visitors and teachers should stop them by changing the subject before the child discloses facts which are not their concern.

Gossip is not conversation.

———

Teach children to speak with deference to adults.

———

Teach children to carry on conversations with people of different ages. Play it as a game.

———

When children lack training in conversation, they find conversations very painful. If they are prepared, they learn to enjoy speaking with people of all ages.

———

Teach the children to say "Please" and "Thank you" on all occasions. Also teach them to say "Pardon?" instead of "What?"

———

Many children have difficulty speaking. Sometimes the causes are physical. These cases require medical help. More often the cause of poor speech is the lack of adequate training.

———

The child needs endless opportunities to develop his ability to communicate. Parents should *talk* to the baby before he begins to talk.

———

Parents should be pleasant and assuring and then wait for a response of mood (not words) on the part of the child.

Parents should carry the baby about the house giving names to objects and names to movements that they make. The child absorbs this instruction even though he is not yet able to express it.

When the child begins to make sounds, the parents listen carefully to see if the child is forming the consonants correctly. They make the sound correctly but show *no* concern about any imperfections.

When the child begins to talk, he may have difficulty in making some consonant sounds.

The consonant sounds which bother some children can be corrected in the following way:

1) *l*—llll which they call *y*—yuh (yook instead of look)

> To get the correct sound, have the child lift the tip of the tongue to the roof of the mouth.
>
> Practice with the words: *l*et, *l*ittle, *l*ook, *l*ong.

2) *m*—mmmm (a hum)

> Close the lips. The feeling is saying it on the outside of the mouth, as in mmmm, good. Mmmm should not be confused with nnnn , lips open.

3) *p*—puh

> If the child continues to make the sound of *b*-buh instead of *p*-puh, place the eraser of a pencil in the center of the upper lip. This helps the child to locate the muscles which must be used to make the sound.

4) *r*—rrrr

> When the child says the sound of *w* for the sound of *r*, have him place his hands on his cheeks and push his cheeks and lips forward. Accompanied by a roaring sound, the child will produce the correct sound of *r*.

5) *s*—suh

> Lisping is not necessary. It occurs when the child sep-
> arates the teeth and lets the tongue come forth between
> the teeth. Have the pupil close his teeth firmly and say:
> *s*it, *s*at, *s*illy, *s*unny—five times. This exercise should
> be continued several times daily until the tongue muscle
> gets strong enough to keep the tongue behind the teeth
> when they are allowed to open.

6) *w*—Do not use the upper lip when saying *w*.

> *wh* requires the forward movement of the lips. The *h* gives
> a blowing sound (hwuh).

7) *th*—thuh

> The sound *th* is difficult for some children. It is made by
> pushing a stiff tongue forward—past the open teeth—
> and then drawing the tongue back quickly. Practice it
> with the following words: this, that, than, them, there.

> When *th* is on the end of the word, pronounce the word
> as if it were a two-syllable word.

> fifth (fif—th) width (wid—th)
> sixth (six—th) length (leng—th)

> Soon the word will flow into one syllable.

Some children who have difficulty in speaking have emotional
problems which can be helped.

Tensions can make the speech hurried—words tend to tumble
over each other, and clarity of speech disappears.

Tensions cause speech problems. They should be avoided or decreased. Some parents live at a very high pitch. They fill the air with all kinds of tension.

Parents whose interests are mainly social often radiate tensions.

Parents who are rivalrous for their children put great pressure on them.

Critical parents create an atmosphere of tension. Children who live in a tense atmosphere often develop stuttering.

Stuttering is most certainly the result of tension.

TEACH YOUR CHILD THE REAL VALUES IN LIFE

Children must be helped to realize that work is a real friend.

Work orients the life, gives one the opportunity to make a contribution to life, and prevents one's experience from being aimless.

A child needs to learn that he must achieve in his work to the best of his ability in order to enjoy a sense of accomplishment and satisfaction.

It is not wise to allow a child to indulge himself. A child needs to realize that he must earn the right to special privileges and pleasures. Unless he does, he is robbed of the true satisfaction which is the natural companion of a just reward.

———

Work for the youngster is school. He owes it to himself and his family to work diligently during the school years.

———

A wise boy or girl acquires enough foundation in school to equip him to pursue whichever course he may choose when he reaches adulthood.

———

A child often has an innate sense about people who are not good for him.

When a child expresses a dislike for a teacher, family friend, or acquaintance, do not tell the child that the person is a "nice person." Just say, "We do not talk about people." Otherwise, you will destroy the child's natural sense of protection.

———

Do not force your child to play with a child or children who do not appeal to him. If the children belong to close friends, take all of them to some form of entertainment when it is necessary for them to be together.

———

Let your children settle their own quarrels with other children. Do not defend your child; let the children settle it instead. If some one of your child's playmates is too rough, do not allow them to play together.

Teach your child to reserve the word *friend* for a *real friend*. Help him to use the words classmate, playmate, and neighbor. Avoid the words boy friend and girl friend.

———

Teach children to admire the achievements of others. If they begrudge success to others, they should be helped to overcome this ungenerous spirit.

———

Why don't we dwell on superiority? That would be productive!

———

Teach children to admire—not destroy.

———

Parents should speak of *lucky* in the sense of fortunate, and call the child's attention to little incidents which are examples of luck. This attitude dispels the tendency to complain.

———

Teach your child that popularity is fickle, and it has no substance. Being admired is preferable. To be truly admired you must retain your individuality, be true to yourself and your standards, show stamina and perseverance, and accomplish at least a good part of what you set out to do.

———

Work always toward the development of a good sense of humor.

The person with a real sense of humor has a balanced view-point and an optimistic outlook, while the person who lacks a sense of humor seldom has a balanced viewpoint because he is pessimistic in outlook.

DO NOT OVERLOOK CHARACTER FAULTS

Parents should discuss character faults with their child only when both parent and child are in a calm mood. Together they should set out to overcome this fault.

———

Parents must be quick to give the child a sign of approval when they see him trying to overcome his faults.

———

Parents should never be mawkish in their approval. Be matter of fact.

———

Character defects that must be dispelled are pride, stubborn-ness, lack of sympathy, unfairness, exaggerations, stinginess, and secretiveness.

———

Eliminate stinginess! It indicates a personality which thinks only of itself, lacks empathy, lacks self-criticism, lacks the ability to see itself as others see it.

———

Stinginess cramps the soul.

To stop stinginess when the child is very young, give the child a toy, let him play with the toy for a few minutes, and then indicate that you want it back. Smile approvingly and say, "Thank you." Your approval will always work wonders! As he gets older, give him a box of candy, and have him pass it around. Keep repeating the act of giving. Talk to him about helping others, about sharing.

———

Achieve generosity via mental training in order to submerge the instinct to keep.

———

Worrying qualities—anxiety, apprehension, distrust, despair —weigh heavily on a youngster.

Unworthy qualities—deceit, dishonesty, cruelty, animosity— disfigure a child's life.

Unless you succeed in helping your child to dispel these detrimental qualities, his life experience will not be a happy one.

———

Parents must realize the price a child will pay for character faults and do everything in their power to help him overcome them.

HELP YOUR CHILD TO DEVELOP THE QUALITIES OF DISPOSITION WHICH MAKE LIFE PLEASANT

Cultivate:

An obliging quality which is the willingness to do for others when the need is obvious or the request is made;

A *genial attitude* which creates a pleasantness in social relationships;

A *sunny quality* which brings radiance into the atmosphere;

An optimistic viewpoint which is a healthy attitude toward events and life;

Generosity of spirit and of material things. Try frequently to have the child develop the impulse to give. If the child has a willingness to give, rejoice.

Help him to acquire:

An ability to express a difference of opinion without causing enmity;

The technique of asking questions instead of making brusque remarks;

The courtesy to be a sincerely good listener because of a feeling of empathy and a good sense of humor;

Cordiality toward all persons with whom he comes in contact.

An accumulation of these qualities will produce a person who will be considered charming and a friend of man.

All of the desirable qualities are inherent within *every* child. They are God-given. It is the job of parents and teachers to recognize the presence of these qualities and to help awaken, stir, and develop them.

———

Remember that the positive qualities of loyalty, honesty, friendship, and reliability, enoble the child's life.

ENCOURAGE A SENSE OF GOOD SPORTSMANSHIP!

Good sportsmanship is a quality which extends into daily experiences and helps the child in all his relationships with his associates.

Everyone admires a good sport—a person who can keep his equilibrium whether he is winning or losing—a *gracious* winner or loser.

———

Some parents wish to excuse slow work by saying that the child is a perfectionist. Isn't he really being a poor sport? Isn't he unwilling to accept the mark for the limited work he has achieved?

Is it fair to make all the more industrious children wait for the child who just takes his time? No! This merely aids the child in his refusal to admit his shortcomings.

This behavior is not the behavior of a perfectionist; it is the behavior of a poor sport.

———

When rivalry and winning have not been over-stressed, it is easier to help the child see the truth.

If a child has a tendency to cry when he loses, the parents should help him to brace himself before the game begins. They do not stress the winning. They stress the interest and fun of the game. They help him to win without an annoying display of elation or to lose without being overly concerned.

———

Parents should provide simple games. A clear distinction must be made between just playing and playing games. Games require at least one opponent and a contest.

The child should be encouraged to enjoy the game for the game's sake. Over-emphasis on winning the game can be detrimental.

———

The nervous strain which accompanies the necessity of winning is undesirable. It leads to unattractive social relations and should not be encouraged.

BUILD FOR YOUR CHILD A WEALTH OF BACKGROUND INFORMATION

Before a child can be prepared for the academic organization of thought, he must acquire the ability to organize the many facets of the world around him.

———

Build background information sequentially. Concepts that are sophisticated beyond the maturity level of the child tend to make him into a "midget adult" who cannot function comfortably in either the adult's world or the child's.

From the beginning, a child should be getting an idea of the classification of foods, clothing, furniture, animals, trees, flowers, boats, and all manner of things.

———

With the baby you begin with a general term such as bird. Then with time and understanding, the names of the best known birds replace the general term. This procedure should be used with flowers, animals, trees, fruits, vegetables, boats, and various other classifications.

———

The different kinds of furniture and furnishings within the home should be given their proper names.

———

Children should experience having household pets where possible.

A child should be helped to overcome fear of tame cats and dogs.

Of course the child should have the nature of the animal explained to him. He should be warned against abusing an animal. This is another area in which a child must learn fair play.

———

The parents should take the young children beyond the confines of the homes, and they should learn the names of different buildings and become familiar with the neighborhood.

In the grocery store, the parents should call the child's attention to the different kinds of cheese, meats, vegetables, crackers, breads, desserts, and talk with the children about their uses.

Widen your child's horizons.

Take the younger ones to see the woods, the farm, the country, the city, the zoo. Prepare the child for these outings. Explain the behavior which is required of him.

If the child is young, hold his hand. Do not permit him to wander about. Visit with him as you walk or ride along. Teach him to be observing.

Always keep in mind that you must work to develop your child's powers of perception.

Parents should always try to instill a sense of appreciation of the beautiful in life.

Beginning in babyhood, children should be awakened to beauty. Introduce the word *pretty* as early as possible. Apply it to flowers, to birds, to all things that are pretty. Point out the beauty of the trees, of the grass—of nature. Point out the beauty of household objects, of clothes, of animals. Show them pictures which are pretty and those which are not pretty. Ask the child to point to the pretty one. Obviously enjoy beauty yourself.

The beautiful sights of nature should be pointed out to children. Whether the beautiful sight is a sunset, the color of the ocean on a gray day, shadow patterns on the wall, a look of surprise on a child's face, or light reflected in a raindrop, it should be enjoyed with a sense of delight.

Build an awareness of and an appreciation for nature.

———

Help your child to notice and enjoy the infinite variety with which nature surrounds us.

———

Notice the weather. On a beautiful day, you might say, "It is a lovely day. It makes us all feel happy, doesn't it?" After a rain enjoy the freshness of the atmosphere.

———

When the child sits looking at a beautiful scene or sunset, the parent asks gently how it makes the child feel. If the child lacks words, the parent might ask another question or two. The questions generally free the child so that he can answer with imagination and depth.

AWAKEN IN YOUR CHILD AN APPRECIATION OF THE WISDOM AND BEAUTY IN GOOD LITERATURE

A taste for *good* literature is the goal of reading.

———

Casual reading has its place, but the teacher and the parent should try to equip the child with fundamental reading skills so that he will be willing to develop an understanding of the real purpose and technique of reading.

———

Parents should read to the child daily, and they should show enthusiasm. It is their responsibility to awaken the young child to the world of books and to create a sense of the importance of reading.

In the selection of books, parents should be careful to see that they are well written and on a wide variety of subjects.

———

Parents should read books which are suitable for the child's age and maturity. Books above the child's grasp encourage inattentiveness. Books below the child's interests create boredom and will build a dislike for literature.

———

The parents should follow a recommended reading list. Parents, when reading to the children, should watch their diction, word grouping, and emphasis.

———

Books play a large role in the development of a speaking, as well as a reading, vocabulary. Any book that is worth reading is worth reading again and again.

———

Avoid the mistake of reading advanced material to children because you consider them to be very advanced or very intelligent.

Regardless of ability, it is necessary to give everyone a solid and sequential literary background. When you present ideas that are beyond the maturity of the child, you develop his palate beyond his ability to produce and make what he can produce so far below his taste that eventually he will refuse to try.

———

Children should be encouraged to listen to stories of literary value over and over again.

The parent encourages the child to visualize the story as it is read in order to develop the *mental image*. Ask him what he sees in his head. Help him to form his mental picture by telling him what you see in your mind's eye. Be brief so that he can embellish in his own way.

––––––

Always encourage the child to tell the story in order to develop the ability to communicate, and ask him to select special parts of the story which appeal to him. *Do not correct the child when he is doing his best.*

––––––

When a child makes an error in the telling of a story, the parents should agree with the idea and, in a spirit of enjoyment, state the idea correctly. Weave it in several times. Do not correct the error. A great deal of help should be given until the child gains the ability to tell the story alone.

––––––

The parents should set the example of reading good literature. Each one should set aside a short period daily for his own reading.

––––––

The child should have many opportunities to observe his parents reading and enjoying it.

––––––

When there are children of different ages, books of different levels should be used. Parents should continue to read to their older children as well as to their younger children. If parents do not read to the older children, they begin to pull away from parental guidance. Younger children should have a separate time for books which they enjoy.

Literary companionship helps to create a lasting bond between parents and child.

———

It is true that school age children should have books which they read themselves, but parents should read these books when the children are not around so that they can communicate with the child about the content of the book. In a discussion of his book, the child should be given the opportunity to lead the conversation. However, the parents should ask questions and be responsive.

If the child shows no reaction, the parent may say the wrong thing in order to awaken the child. Be sure he is *thinking* as he reads.

———

Do not allow your children to read just to be reading. Passive reading is as dangerous to a child as sitting and staring at the television screen without thinking. Passive reading is deadening to the brain.

———

There is nothing wrong with television except in the selection of poor programs and in watching them without having to be responsible for making it a worthy use of time. If you are going to allow your children to watch television, watch it with them, ask them questions about what they see, and force them to think and evaluate.

———

The reading of poetry is as essential as the reading of prose.

———

Poetry breathes beauty into the commonplace and lifts the soul.

Poems should be memorized and enjoyed within the family life.

———

Parents should read poetry to their children. Start with the nursery rhymes, then add other poems frequently. Strive to develop a sense of rhythm.

———

In teaching young children the nursery rhymes, the first step is to let the child complete the rhyming word. Then the child should be encouraged to recite the whole rhyme. Please avoid a sing-song recitation!

———

Every parent should have a book of poems for children on his library shelf. These poems should have a variety of interests. Humorous ones should be included, too.

———

Parents should memorize poems and recite them with their children.

In the reciting of poetry, parents should not be exacting about complete accuracy. When a word escapes the child, just put it in. Criticism in any form spoils the pleasure for everyone.

MAKE MUSIC A NATURAL PART OF YOUR CHILD'S LIFE

Many times when words avail not, the language of music can reach out with a message of comfort and hope, give a lift to the spirits, soothe the troubled soul, or replenish the heart with joy.

————

Parents should begin to sing to the baby when he is very young. It is wise to sing one little lullaby over and over again. Gradually the baby will begin to hum along. This constant repetition will steady the pitch, and the child will gradually gain an accuracy of pitch.

————

Children who are musical can sing at a very early age. Teach them.

————

Do not neglect the children who are not musical. By constant repetition the child's ear and voice will improve.

If a parent cannot sing, a record of a simple song is helpful. Even a music box is helpful.

————

The child should learn the songs to which nursery rhymes are sung. Songs should never be limited to the popular songs of the day. The well-beloved songs, which are the heritage of the nation, be they patriotic, religious, or fun-loving in nature, should be taught to every child.

The child should hear short selections of the great masters. The child should be encouraged to hum along with the music. Different composition forms should be included to give the child a concept of the variety of musical forms.

Different musical instruments, too, should become familiar to children.

Formal music lessons are most successfully begun when a child is eight years old. The child should have a deep desire to begin music lessons and should accept totally the responsibility for practice. Children can be expected to carry this responsibility only if the parents display obvious interest in and appreciation for every step of accomplishment. However, if with this support the student does not assume responsibility for his practice, lessons should be discontinued until he is willing to do so.

If a child shows musical ability, a desire to study, and the responsibility needed to practice, he should have the support of his parents in his pursuit.

INTRODUCE YOUR CHILDREN TO THE BEAUTY OF FINE ART

Parents should provide opportunities for their young children to become acquainted with a few fine paintings and works of art. Prints are easily obtainable, inexpensive, and good, but museums afford the thrill of seeing the real masterpiece. Gradually a few more paintings and art works are added — then more and more until the child has a wide acquaintance-ship with famous works of art.

In order to have children enjoy the paintings, sculpture, and various works, parents should enjoy them, too. There must be no pressure.

———

Parents should realize that the mere naming of paintings and artists is not the goal of acquainting children with works of art. The purpose is to develop the sensitivity of the child to beauty.

PROVIDE YOUR CHILD WITH THE BEST EDUCATION POSSIBLE

The process of education should equip the individual with the ability to analyze, evaluate, and classify all of the information that comes to him.

The purpose of education is to teach individuals to *THINK* and to develop good judgment.

The acquisition of these skills relies on a thorough curriculum that interrelates all subject matter in a sequential manner and is continued from grade to grade.

———

A collection of miscellaneous facts is *not* an education.

———

Sound education enables one to understand, organize, and apply everything he knows.

———

Real education develops sound judgment and requires practical application of knowledge in all aspects of learning and in every phase of life.

True education includes an adherence to fine character traits and worthy citizenship. It enables the student to see life in true focus and orients the individual to the real values of life.

———

People used to be ashamed if they did not know anything. Now the attitude seems to be, "Who cares?" Do not be fooled by what seems to be; it is merely a cover-up for having never been taught.

———

Children wake up and have a terrific desire to learn at about five and one-half years of age. If that desire is not captured, they go back to sleep, and the job of reawakening a desire to learn becomes increasingly difficult with each passing day.

———

A child's first few years in school are far more important than any others.

———

During the first few years in school, a child must master the basic skills, or he will have no foundation on which to build.

———

He must master reading, writing, spelling, arithmetic, and develop excellent work habits. He must learn to think, and to organize, and outline the subject matter which he reads. With this background, he will have a foundation on which all the other scholastic achievements can be based.

Parents should be sure that the school in which they enroll their children is one that provides the children with this vital background in order to secure their future academic work.

Parents who save for a college education while they neglect the early school years make a grave mistake.

If a student has a sound academic background, good work habits, and the will to succeed, there will be no limit to the opportunities readily available for him in the continuation of his education.

On the other hand, if a student has a poor academic background, which is inevitably coupled with non-existent study habits and discouragement, all the money in the world cannot help him in college.

————

The learning process requires *self-disciplined concentration* and acute perception.

Parents should be aware of these skills and should prepare the children to meet these requirements.

Parents, if you will send to school children who will listen when directions are given to them, who will carry out the instructions given, who are courteous to adults and to playmates, and who have been awakened to the joy of learning, you can rely on the fact that their school experience will be pleasant and rewarding.

However, if you send to school children who do not listen when directions are given to them, who do not carry out the instructions given, or who are discourteous to adults and to playmates, you will find that these children have difficulty making an adjustment to school.

Parents should give the child the feeling that education is a great privilege.

———

Attendance at school should be regular. Every day missed is knowledge lost.

———

Do not take the child out of school for unnecessary trips. The young child will not remember what he sees. Travel does not mean as much to the child as it does to you. All too often his view is composed mainly of shoe laces.

———

Do not try to decide the level of the class for your child. To you he is very talented and advanced. Fortunately, most parents have that same opinion about *their* offspring! On the other hand, do not limit him either.

If your child is able to perform in a superior way within the group, the teacher will advance him. Do not try to push your child.

———

Maturity, not memory, is the gauge of the child's ability to function with older groups.

———

A child who is pushed is going to be a nervous child. If you love your child, guard his nervous system. There is neither health nor happiness for the child who becomes nervous.

———

Many children are being driven to get marks. Marks, not knowledge and understanding, become all important. This is an utter disregard of true value.

Do not make your child over-anxious about his marks. Do not criticize him. Let him progress naturally, and don't bribe him!

When your child comes home with poor marks, say, "Well, that teacher doesn't know a smart one when she sees one!" Then check with the school to see where the trouble lies and together seek a solution.

Do not expect immediate success. Be thrilled by gradual progress.

Be interested in the child's school life, but stay away from school. Do not take up the teacher's time with unnecessary chatting. A good teacher will send for you if she needs your advice or help.

Do not allow your child to use you as a buffer between himself and the teacher.

Do not do your children's homework. Good schools do not grade parents. If you correct your child's homework, the teacher will not know where he needs help.

A conscientious teacher will give you some suggestions about home help *if* she thinks that it will benefit your child.

Parents can support the school's efforts to teach children in many ways that do not interfere. Continue to build background information. Respect the national holidays and teach children some additional facts about them.

Widen your child's knowledge when you are riding or traveling. Establish which direction is north, south, east, and west. Help him to be interested in maps.

GIVE YOUR CHILD THE GREAT STRENGTH OF RELIGIOUS FAITH

Parents should present their own religious faith to their children.

Regardless of your religious affiliation, begin early to establish the habit of a short daily prayer in the morning and in the evening which will awaken a child to an awareness of the presence of God.

Bible stories are a part of the rightful heritage of our children, and many of them can be told to very young children. As they grow older, children will enjoy the more difficult stories and should be encouraged to tell the simpler ones to younger children.

At a very early age the Golden Rule should be taught to the child through demonstration. This is the child's introduction to empathy.

An important lesson to teach the child is to play life the long way. Momentary pleasure is tempting, but it is soon over.

The person who can forego momentary pleasures in order to reach higher goals is the person who is playing life the long way.

———

Help your child to realize that only in his relationship with God can he experience true completeness.

———

From early childhood the parents should be giving a child strength in making wise decisions. He must be given answers for the scoffing and belittling that he will hear, such as the denial of life's values and the disrespect for parents and their ideas.

Parents should talk about the attitudes which await them. If the child is prepared for them and has values of his own, he will not be overly influenced by them. He will not feel called upon to defend his own convictions, nor will he be shocked by the force of the arguments used against the standards of upright living.

———

The question of morality should be a familiar topic in the home. The temptations should be discussed, and the child should be encouraged to ask questions as frequently as necessary until he rids his emotions of uncertainty or rebellion and can plan a life which will be the fulfillment of the real desires of his heart.

Wise parents never allow themselves to project in a specific sense just what a child should be and do in the future, for each one is fitted for his own special pursuit or activity. But they do constantly keep in mind the image they envision for the child concerning standards of integrity, happiness, and success.

Gradually this image establishes itself in the mind of the young person, and as he grows in his own way and direction, it becomes an integral part of him.

Parents must keep an optimistic viewpoint of the future and let the child know that they expect him to be the finest type of person—living to his full potential. Speak as though it were already a reality.

———

As a young person arrives at a conviction regarding his goal in life, parents should show interest. Sometimes parents can help to provide opportunities necessary to the accomplishment of the young person's goal. These should be provided but often without definite requirements. If the parent demands too much, too early, the young person is liable to tire or rebel.

———

When one has helped his child to develop stamina, self-control, perseverance, and interest, he will have enabled the child to attain the goals of his heart's desire, because that young person will have the strength of character to resist the attractions which would have had momentary appeal and would have prevented him from attaining the higher goal.

Keep the child's mind on higher thoughts.

CONCLUSION

When the basic values of life, discussed within this little book, have been woven into the child's life experience, they will act as a bulwark against the disillusionments of life.

All of the sound values and all of the skills do not lead to a somber existence. Rather they clear the vision, lighten the spirit, lift the mood, bring balance to life, and fill it with joy, humor, whimsy, and radiance.

If the child learns to play fair in all his relationships, and builds his life on the rule of cause and effect, he will experience *life triumphant!*

His outlook on life will be cheery, and his heart will be filled with sunshine.

What a contribution *that* person can make to his world and to everyone in it!

THE END